MICROSOFT SURFACE LAPTOP GO USER GUIDE

The Beginner to Expert Guide to Master the Microsoft Surface Laptop GO

Raphael Stone

Copyright © 2020 by Raphael Stone- All rights reserved.

No part of this publication windows 10 2019 guide may be reproduced, stored in a retrieval system or transmitted in any form or by any means, electronic, mechanical, photocopying, recording, and scanning without permission in writing by the author.

The information provided herein is stated to be truthful and consistent, in that any liability, in terms of inattention or otherwise, by any usage or abuse of any policies, processes, or directions contained within is the solitary and utter responsibility of the recipient reader. Under no circumstances will any legal responsibility or blame be held against the publisher for any reparation, damages, or monetary losses due to the information herein, either directly or indirectly. Respective authors own all copyrights not held by the publisher. The information herein is offered for informational purposes solely, and is universal as so. The presentation of the information is without contract or any type of guarantee assurance. The trademarks that are used are without any consent, and the publication of the trademark is without permission or backing by the trademark owner. All trademarks and brands within this book, except are for clarifying purposes only and are owned by the owners themselves, not affiliated with this document. Printed in the united states of America

© **2020 by Raphael Stone**

Gm Publishing House
9577, Creek rd, Chino Hills
CA 91709
California
USA

Contents

Introduction 1

How to Use Your Surface PC as a Portable Display 10

Using Surface with iPhone, iCloud, and iTunes 18

Get iTunes for your Surface 18

Set up iCloud for Windows 19

Sync your iPhone and Surface using OneDrive 19

Sign in to OneDrive on Surface 20

Sign in to OneDrive on iPhone 20

Get photos from your iPhone to your Surface 20

Upload your photos to OneDrive 39

See your photos on Surface 40

Use Office apps on your Surface and iPhone 40

Edit your Office documents on your iPhone and Surface
41

See your email accounts and calendars in one place with Microsoft Outlook 42

Browse the web on your iPhone, continue on your Surface... 42

Link your iPhone to your Surface 43

Send a webpage from your iPhone to your Surface 43

Set up your Surface.. 44

Set up Windows Hello 44

Protect your device 45

Power cord care 45

Take care of your touch screen 47

How to use your Surface Pen 48

Use the top button of your pen 2

Use top button shortcuts 3

Ultimate Tips to Max Out Microsoft Surface Battery Life 4

How to charge Surface Pro 7 via USB-C? 24

How to Configure Surface Pro UEFI/BIOS Settings.... 25

How to easily disable adaptive contrast on Surface Pro 7 and Surface Laptop 3 27

How to disable adaptive contrast with 29
   Intel's Store app 29

How to Check Your Surface Pro Device Information via UEFI settings? 30

How to Configure Device Boot Order on the new Surface Pro 30

How to Manage Device Components on Surface Pro ... 31

How to change your Surface Pro Date and Time via Surface UEFI? 33

How to Protect UEFI settings with a password on Surface Pro 34

Customizing Windows 10 35
   How to change the desktop background 36
   Setting up a desktop slideshow 37

How to change the color accent 39
Controlling transparency effects 41
Adding colors to Windows 10 elements 42
Choosing a color mode 43
How to customize the Lock screen 44
Setting up a Lock screen slideshow 46
Controlling Lock screen app notifications 48
How to apply a theme 50
How to customize the Start menu 52
Customizing Live Tiles 56
A Windows 7 Start menu look 60
How to customize the taskbar 61
Customizing the notification area 64
Disabling My People 66
Optimizing the taskbar space 67

Microsoft Edge Web Browser 69
What You Need to Know About Edge 70
Getting Started with Edge 71
Turning Off Flash in Edge 76

Introduction

The Surface Laptop Go is a new flavor of Surface. It's not to be confused with the Surface Go (Microsoft's budget-minded detachable 2-in-1, now on the **Surface Go 2** generation), the Surface Pro (the "original" Surface 2-in-1, now on the **Surface Pro 7**), the **Surface Book** (the company's top-shelf detachable laptop), or the various Surface Laptop 3 models. In brief, as its hybrid of a name implies, it's a classic clamshell model like the Surface Laptops, but smaller and cheaper, like the Surface Go models.

The Surface Laptop Go is petite as modern laptops go, with a 12.4-inch display, but its physical design matches the rest of the Surface Laptop 3 family, which includes larger, pricier 13.5-inch and 15-inch versions. The design includes an aluminum display lid and a polycarbonate base, available in your choice of three colors: Ice Blue, Sandstone, and

Platinum. The entire package feels sturdy, well-engineered, and fitting of a laptop that costs more than its $699 asking price.

In addition to being easy on your budget, the Surface Laptop Go will also please your shoulders when you carry it around. It measures 0.62 by 10.95 by 8.1 inches (HWD), and it weighs just 2.45 pounds. Those numbers put it at the svelte end of the **ultraportable class** of laptops. By comparison, the **13.5-inch Surface Laptop 3** is 0.57 by 12.1 by 8.8 inches and 2.83 pounds, while the **Apple MacBook Air** is 0.63 by 11.97 by 8.5 inches and 2.8 pounds.

On the inside, the Surface Laptop Go keeps things simple. There's a single processor option, an Intel Core i5, a clear indication that this laptop is not suited for power users. The $549.99 entry-level configuration of the laptop nets you 4GB of memory and a 64GB eMMC flash storage drive. We recommend stepping up from this configuration, if you can, since those amounts are paltry in today's world of ever-increasing program sizes. (The

Windows 10 operating system alone can take up 20GB or more.)

Instead, most people should opt for the configuration reviewed here, which costs an extra $150, doubles the memory, and replaces the flash storage drive with a 128GB solid-state drive (SSD) that is both more capacious and more capable than the eMMC base option. You can also configure a Surface Laptop Go with 256GB of storage, but you can't go higher than that, so anyone with large local media collections will need to connect an external drive.

Fortunately, the Surface Laptop Go's port selection is well-suited to external connections without requiring adapters, especially for a laptop of its size and price. Microsoft gives you both a rectangular USB Type-A port and a USB-C port, which will let you plug in pretty much any peripheral made in the last few years.

While the USB Type-C port can be used to charge the laptop's battery using a USB-C cable connected to an AC outlet, Microsoft includes a proprietary 39-watt AC adapter with a Surface Connect plug, which connects to a port (dubbed "Surface Connect") on the right side of the Surface Laptop Go.

The Surface Connect port can also support one of a few Microsoft expansion hubs and docks. A 3.5mm headphone jack rounds out the Surface Laptop Go's port selection, while the wireless-connection hardware supports 802.11ax (Wi-Fi 6) and Bluetooth 5.0.

A Screen With an Unusual Resolution

Yes, the Surface Laptop Go's screen is more than an inch smaller than the screen of the smallest Surface Laptop 3, but many people won't find this to be a drawback. For one thing, a smaller screen enables the laptop to be slimmer and lighter. Also, the Surface Laptop Go maintains the relatively rare 3:2 screen aspect ratio of the rest of the Surface Laptop family. This is taller and narrower than the customary 16:9 orientation used on laptops, which means that you can see more of a vertical document, like a web page, or more lines of an Excel spreadsheet before you have to scroll down.

The only potential downside to the Surface Laptop Go's screen is its relatively low native resolution of 1,536 by 1,024 pixels, which makes for a density of 148 pixels per inch (ppi). Given the screen size, this is essentially equivalent to a full HD resolution, which is adequate for a sub-$1,000 laptop, but it's significantly lower than the resolutions of both the Surface Laptop 3 13-Inch (2,256 by 1,504 pixels) and the MacBook Air (2,560 by 1,600 pixels). The difference means noticeably grainy text at times when viewing the Surface Laptop Go from a comfortable distance of two feet. Still, the screen is otherwise high-quality, with 10-point touch support and more than enough maximum brightness to be viewed in a sunlit-flooded living room.

Above the display, there's a 720p front-facing video camera. With so many people now spending significant portions of their day on video calls as they work from home, it's a bit disappointing that Microsoft didn't elect to outfit the Surface Laptop Go with a 1080p webcam. The 720p one is adequate, but it delivers slightly noisy picture quality even when your room is decently lit. The camera also lacks face recognition sign-ins via Windows Hello, a feature that Microsoft has heavily promoted and which is available on nearly all of the company's other Windows devices. The omission of the IR sensors required for Windows Hello and a 1080p camera are likely cost-saving measures.

Instead of face recognition, the Surface Laptop Go includes a power button that doubles as a fingerprint reader, which still allows you to sign in to your Windows account without typing a password. This is a familiar feature on Mac laptops, and I actually find it to be more reliable than face recognition at logging me in every time, even if it's not as futuristic as the face recognition that is now commonplace on phones and Windows laptops.

A Generously Sized Touchpad

The power button/fingerprint reader combo is nestled into the top row of the keyboard on the $699 model (the $549.99 configuration lacks a fingerprint reader). The keyboard itself offers the comfortable typing experience that I've come to expect from Surface devices, though unfortunately it lacks key backlighting. Below the keyboard, there's a generously sized touchpad with accurate tracking and a sturdy, refined clicking mechanism.

The Surface Laptop Go's chassis is completely sealed except for a recessed grille next to the display hinge, which spreads across most of the width of the laptop. This grille handles air intake and outflow to cool the internal components, and I did occasionally hear the fan spool up to clearly audible levels when running demanding performance benchmarks. With no other openings, the grille also serves the laptop's speakers, which unfortunately produce loudspeaker-like audio quality that is almost completely devoid of bass. You'll likely want to connect headphones if you plan to watch movies on your Surface Laptop Go.

One technique that laptop manufacturers use to keep prices low on consumer laptops is to install lots of free software trials, which brings in additional revenue. This bloatware is usually useless to the buyer, and it's nice to see that the Surface Laptop Go doesn't have it, apart from the Microsoft 365 trial that comes with all Surface devices. The Surface Laptop Go does ship with Windows 10 S Mode enabled, which limits software installations to apps downloaded from the Microsoft store, but you can easily disable this limitation using Windows Settings and shift the installation over to a full version of Windows 10. (I did this to run our benchmark tests.)

Testing the Surface Laptop Go: A Capable-Enough Core i5

The quad-core Core i5-1035G1 in the Surface Laptop Go is from Intel's 10th Generation "Ice Lake" chip family, introduced at the end of 2019.

It's been superseded by the latest 11th Generation chips unveiled last month (dubbed "Tiger Lake"), but it's still plenty capable. It runs at a low base clock speed of 1GHz to keep power consumption down, but can boost up to 3.8GHz when required. It also features Hyper-Threading, which means each core can handle two instruction threads at once, for a total of eight. Coupled with 8GB of memory and Intel UHD Graphics, this Core i5 was able to handle pretty much every simple task I threw at it without sluggishness, from web browsing with multiple tabs open to writing part of this review in Microsoft Word. When it comes to theoretical performance as measured by our benchmarks, though, it's clear that the Surface Laptop Go's performance is middling against its comparably priced peers. It's slightly faster than the Core i3-equipped Lenovo Yoga C640, but significantly slower on most complex, CPU-intensive tasks than the AMD Ryzen 5-equipped Lenovo IdeaPad Flex 5 14.

How to Use Your Surface PC as a Portable Display

Having a Surface PC? You can configure your Surface as a beautiful portable wireless display or secondary monitor with the mouse, keyboard, touch, and pen support.

Having a dual or multiple monitors setup is really help in multitasking. At my office, I have a triple monitors setup, my main Surface Book display, a 29-inch ultrawide, and a 21.5-inch monitor on either side. With that setup, I can view multiple websites up to 6 websites side by side for doing research, writing articles, and doing many other things.

When I work outside my office, I also have my own portable multiple monitors setup. I don't have a portable monitor, but instead, I have used my Surface 3 as a portable wireless display and it works pretty well for web browsing and most activities.

In this guide, I will walk you through the steps to connect and configure your Surface PCs as a portable wireless display.

1 Preparing your Surface PCs

Before you continue, make sure your both Surface PCs meet the following requirements:

- Running Windows 10 with Anniversary Update or later.

- Connecting to the same network. This feature will work on either a wired network or wireless network. However, if you want the best performance, connect your both Surface PCs to the same wired network via USB to Gigabit Ethernet adapter.

- Surface PCs with the Miracast protocol Support. Fortunately, all Surface lineup except the original Surface RT support this protocols.

In this scenario, I will use my Surface Book as the main PC and a Surface 3 as a portable monitor just like the picture above. Let's get started!

2 Configuring a Surface PC (Surface 3) as a Portable Monitor

To configure your Surface PC (Surface 3) as a wireless display do the following:

1. Open Settings.

2. Click on System.

3. Click on Projecting to this PC.

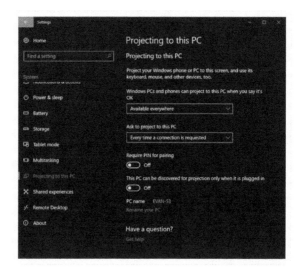

4. Select Available everywhere or Available everywhere on secure networks from the first option.

5. Select First time only or Every time a connection is requested from the second option. If you don't want to confirm every time you connect, choose the First time only option.

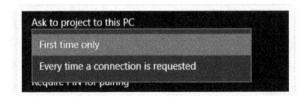

6. Turn on the Required PIN for pairing, if you need an extra protection.

7. Make sure you turn off the "This PC can be discovered for projection only

when it is plugged in as you will use your Surface PC as a portable display.

8. Finally, you will need to confirm Yes when you project from another computer to this PC.

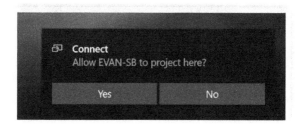

3 Projecting the Surface PC (Surface Book) to a Wireless Display (Surface 3)

Once you have configured your Surface PC (Surface 3) to accept projection, On your main PC (Surface

Book) do the follConnec

1. Open **Action Center**.

2. Click **Connect** button.

3. Click the name of remote wireless display PC (Surface 3) you want to project. You may need to confirm the connection on another PC (Surface 3) depending on your

configuration. If the connection fails, you will need to try again.

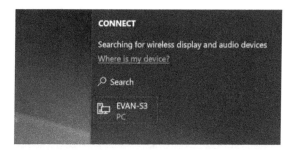

4. Once connected, Toggle the "Allow input from a keyboard or mouse connected to this display", if you also want to use the remote computer (Surface 3)'s mouse, keyboard, touch, and pen input on your main PC (Surface Book).

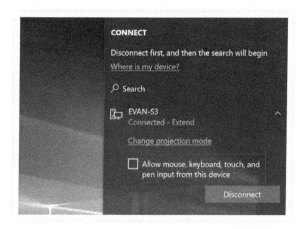

5. You can also change the projection mode just like a real connected monitor, by clicking on Change projection mode or just press Win + P on your keyboard.

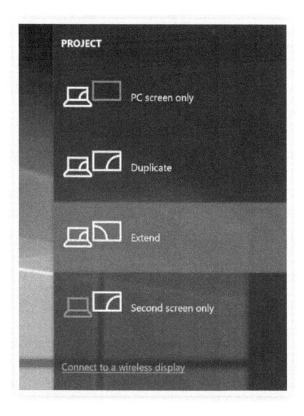

6. Finally, when you finish your work click Disconnect to stop your connection.

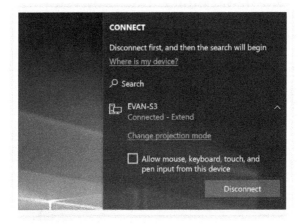

Using Surface with iPhone, iCloud, and iTunes

Your iPhone and Surface work great together. You can use Apple or Microsoft apps and services to connect your devices. Get your pictures, files, and contacts anywhere, with whatever device you use.

Get iTunes for your Surface

With your Surface, you can purchase, download, and stream music from iTunes. You can also sync your iOS devices to your Surface using iTunes.

Set up iCloud for Windows

If you're already using iCloud, you can keep using it to sync your photos, contacts, and bookmarks to your Surface.

1. On your Surface, download iCloud for Windows from the Microsoft store.

2. Install iCloud for Windows, then restart your device.

3. ICloud will open and ask you to sign in. If you don't see it, go to **Start,** search for **iCloud**, and then select it.

4. Sign in with your Apple ID.

5. Choose what you want to sync to your Surface and select apply.

Sync your iPhone and Surface using OneDrive

OneDrive syncs photos and files from your iPhone to your Surface. You need to sign in to your Microsoft account first, but any updates or changes you make in OneDrive will appear on both your devices.

Sign in to OneDrive on Surface

1. Select **Start** > **Settings** > **Accounts** > **E mail & app accounts** > **Add an account**.

2. Sign in with your Microsoft account and follow the prompts.

Sign in to OneDrive on iPhone

1. Get the OneDrive app from the Apple App Store.

2. In the OneDrive app, sign in with your Microsoft account, then follow the instructions.

Get photos from your iPhone to your Surface

The OneDrive app can automatically upload

photos taken on your iPhone. Your uploaded photos can be seen on your Surface too.

Upload your photos to OneDrive

1. On your iPhone, get the OneDrive app from the Apple App Store.

2. In the OneDrive app, sign in with your Microsoft account.

3. Do one of the following:

- If this is your first time signing in, select **Start Camera Upload** when asked if you'd like to automatically upload photos you take.

- If you've already signed into the OneDrive app, select **me** > **Settings** > **Camera Upload** and turn on **Camera Upload**. Now, every photo you take with your iPhone will be saved to OneDrive. If you want videos to be saved to OneDrive, make sure **Include Videos** is turned on.

See your photos on Surface

OneDrive is built into Windows 10, so you can get your photos from OneDrive in File Explorer.

1. On your Surface, select **File Explorer** on the taskbar.

2. In **File Explorer,** select **OneDrive on** the left side.

3. Sign in with the same Microsoft account used on your iPhone to link your Surface to OneDrive.

4. Once your OneDrive folders appear, select **Pictures** > **Camera Roll**. Pictures taken on your iPhone will appear and you can open and view them from here.

Use Office apps on your Surface and iPhone

If you need to edit Office documents on your iPhone, stay productive with Office apps. You'll be able to create, edit, and share documents directly from your iPhone and continue working on your Surface.

Edit your Office documents on your iPhone and Surface

When you save your documents to OneDrive, you'll see them on both your Surface and iPhone.

1. Search for Microsoft Office apps in the Apple App Store.

2. Select **Install** next to the following apps:

    - Microsoft Word
    - Microsoft Excel
    - Microsoft PowerPoint
    - Microsoft OneNote

3. Open an app to begin editing documents you saved on OneDrive.

Changes will be saved across devices so you can start work on your iPhone and continue on your Surface.

See your email accounts and calendars in one place with Microsoft Outlook

Stay organized when you use Microsoft Outlook on your iPhone. Get a familiar mail experience when you download Microsoft Outlook from the Apple App Store. Set up Microsoft Outlook so you can:

- Get all your important email in a focused inbox.

- Search contacts and attachments from all your email accounts

- See your calendar appointments and reminders across all your accounts with different views

Browse the web on your iPhone, continue on your Surface

Experience seamless web browsing by linking your iPhone and Surface together. You can open a web page using Microsoft Edge on your iPhone, then continue reading it on your Surface.

Link your iPhone to your Surface

1. On your iPhone, download the Microsoft Edge app from the App Store.

2. Open **Microsoft Edge** on your iPhone. Sign in with your Microsoft account to link it to your Surface.

Send a webpage from your iPhone to your Surface

On your iPhone:

1. On your iPhone, open a webpage in **Microsoft Edge.**

2. In the bottom toolbar, select **Continue on PC**.

3. Send the webpage to your Surface by selecting **Choose a PC to open this now** or **Continue Later**.

- o **Choose a PC to open this now** will let you choose a linked computer that is powered on and connected to the internet.

- o **Continue later** sends the webpage to all of your linked computers for later access. When you're ready, go to **action center** and select the webpage to open it on your Surface.

Set up your Surface

Sign in with a Microsoft account

Get free online storage, an online password reset for your Surface, and more with a Microsoft account. All you need to get started is an email address.

Set up Windows Hello

Get instant access to your Surfacewith Windows Hello. Here's how to set it up:

1. Go

    to Start > Settings > Accounts > Sign- in options.

2. Under **Windows Hello**, select **set up**.

Protect your device

Windows Security is included on your device and provides the latest antivirus protection. Your device will be actively protected from the moment you set it up. It continually scans for malware (malicious software), viruses, and security threats. Updates are downloaded automatically to keep your device safe and protect it from threats.

Power cord care

Power cords, like any other metal wire or cable, can be weakened or damaged if repeatedly twisted or bent in the same spot. Here are a few things you can do to keep your power cord from being damaged:

Avoid twisting or pinching your power cord

Don't wrap your power cord too tightly, especially around the power brick. Instead, wrap it using loose coils rather than tight angles.

Correct: wrapped	Cable	loosely	Incorrect: wrapped	Cable	tightly
			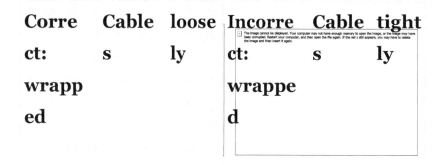		

Inspect your power cord regularly, especially where it joins the power brick avoid pulling on the power cord when unplugging your Surface. Gently removing the connector from the charging port can help prevent damage to your power cord.

Correct: Unplugging gently	Incorrect: Tugging on cord to unplug

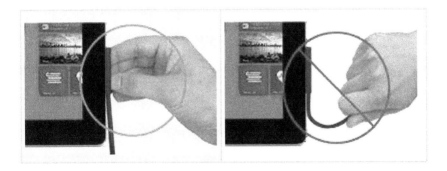

Take care of your touch screen

Scratches, finger grease, dust, chemicals, and sunlight can affect your touchscreen. Here are some tips to protect it:

- Clean frequently. The Surface touchscreen is coated to make it easier to clean. You don't need to rub hard to remove fingerprints or oily spots. Use a soft, line-free cloth (either dry or dampened with water or eyeglass cleaner— never glass or other chemical cleaners) or a screen cleaning wipe to gently wipe the screen.

- Keep it out of the sun. Don't leave your Surface in direct sunlight for a long time.

Ultraviolet light and excessive heat can damage the display.

Keep it covered. Close the cover when you're taking your Surface with you or when you're not using it.

How to use your Surface Pen

Interact with your Surface in new ways using Surface Pen.

Write and draw

- Use your Surface Pen in any app that supports inking.

    Start inking with your pen

- Rest your hand on the screen, like you would on a piece of paper, then start writing. Your Surface is designed to ignore your hand and other inputs while you write. Use the pointer that appears under your pen tip to guide you while you ink.

To erase, turn your pen over and rub the end of your pen over your writing or drawing.

- Enter text with your pen

If you want to write instead of typing on a keyboard, you can use the touch keyboard that appears on the screen.

- Navigate and click using your pen

Your pen can be used throughout Windows, similarly to how you would use a mouse or keyboard. Here are some actions you can start with.

If you want to	Do this with your pen
Click or select	Tap on an item.
Right	Press and hold the side button, then tap on the item.

click	
Drag and drop	Place your pen on an item, and hold it there until the circle around the pointer completes. Then move the item to where you want it to want it to go.
Select multiple items	Press and hold the side button, then drag your pen Over the items you want go select.

Use the top button of your pen

Pair Surface Pen

Your pen uses Bluetooth to pair with your Surface. Here's how:

1. Go to Start > Settings > Devices > Add Bluetooth or other device > Bluetooth.

2. Press and hold the top button of your pen

for 5-7 seconds until the LED flashes white to turn on Bluetooth pairing mode.

3. Select your pen to pair it to your Surface.

Use top button shortcuts

Once your pen is paired, you'll be able to use the top button. The top button does different things depending on how you interact with the button. To change these shortcuts, go to **Start > Settings > Devices > Pen & Windows Ink.**

If you want to	Do this with your pen
Open Microsoft Whiteboard	Click the top button once.
Open Snip & Sketch	Double-click the top button.
Open Sticky Notes	Press and hold the top button.

Ultimate Tips to Max Out Microsoft Surface Battery Life

There are two main factors that reflect battery life on every computer: "Battery Capacity" and "Power Efficiency". There is nothing we can do here with the device's battery capacity as it is already built into your device already. Check out here to see your Surface's battery capacity.

In this section, we will guide you how to tune power settings and system settings to maximize your Surface's power efficiency.

1 Real-time battery discharging monitoring

Before we deep dive into how to max out the battery life on Surface Pro 4 and Surface Book, we need to know how to track battery discharging in your current configuration. By monitoring the battery discharging we are able to know about:

- How much power is used in the whole system in real-time?

- What activities that will use much power to process.

- Compare power usage when you customize your system configuration.

As my experience, BatteryBar is the best battery monitoring tool out there. It has all features that we need to monitor battery discharging in real-time. Below is all the basic real-time battery information that available:

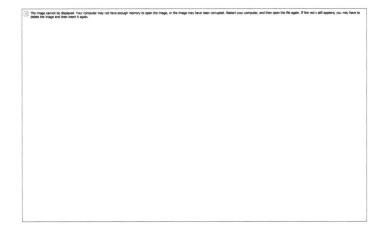

As you can see my current Discharge Rate is 3,539 mW or 3.5W and with 82.9% of battery capacity, so it means that with current system configuration and activities my battery life still remains 6 hours and 16 minutes.

Now you got the idea, to get more battery life you will need to minimize discharge rate as possible. Now it's time to max out your Surface Pro 7 battery life, please check out the following tips:

2 Surface Pro Optimization power plan

Note - I have tested this section on my Surface Book with Windows 10 Fall Creators Update along with Power Slider feature enabled. I can confirm that every power settings you set here are still working normally.

Every Microsoft Surface devices shipped with a predefined power plan called Balanced with very few advanced configurations as below:

Step 1: Turning off Connected Standby feature

The limited power configuration in Advanced Settings because of Connected Standby feature that enabled by default on every Surface devices. In order to create a new power plan with optimized advanced settings, we need to disable connected standby via Registry Editor.

To turn off connected standby:

- On your type cover, press + R
- Type regedit to open Register Editor.

- Now you need to go to HKEY_LOCAL_MACHINE\SYSTEM\Current ControlSet\Control\Power

- Double click on CsEnabled and change Value data from 1 to 0, and click OK.

- Restart your computer to apply these changes to your system.

- After restarting your computer, now you can access the full list of power plans and individual advanced settings.Full List of Power Advanced Settings

Step 2: Notice your default properties of Balanced power plan

Before we move on to create the Surface Pro Optimization power plan, here are all the settings of the Balanced power plan that we will copy for creating our new power plan:

Step 3: Creating a new Surface Pro Optimization power plan

To create the Surface Pro Optimization power plan based on Balanced power plan:

1. Right-click on Start > Control Panel

2. Navigate to Hardware and Sound > Power Options

3. On the left navigation pane, click Create a power plan

4. Type "Surface Pro Optimization" in the Plan name textbox. You can also use whatever name you want here:

Important - You need to reset the value of CsEnabled back to "1" to bring back the Connected Standby feature that allows you to instantly turn on/off your Surface. You will not see all advanced settings but everything you made changes to all power plants will still remain there.

Step 4: How to verify the new power plan settings via Command Prompt

After you turned on back the Connected Standby feature, you will no longer access most advanced power settings from Power Options in control panel you set before. Here is how you can verify those advanced power settings:

3. Optimizing Cortana Settings

Cortana is a Windows 10 voice assistant, she runs in the background at all time to track your activities including speaking, inking, and typing personalization. She uses your internet connection to send those data to the Cortana server, and also synchronize suggestions, reminders, alerts and personalization information for you.

As you can see, those activities will definitely eat up your battery life. If you want to max out your battery life, you need to optimize the Cortana settings to do little things as possible. To do so:

- Click on Cortana icon
- Click the Settings icon
- And turn off all options there

Turn off Cortana completely on Windows 10 anniversary update

Since Windows 10 anniversary, you can't disable Cortana completely via the Settings anymore. To disable Cortana you need to change the Computer Configuration via Local Group Policy Editor.

To do that:

- Click Start and type "gpedit.msc" and press Enter.

- Go to Computer Configuration > Administrative Templates > Windows Components > Search.

- Double-click on Allow Cortana to change the policy.

- Select Disabled.

- Click Apply and OK

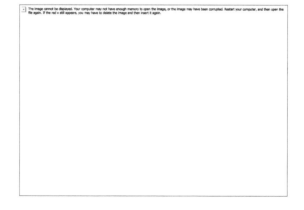

4 Turn off Wi-Fi while asleep

While connected standby is turned on Surface devices, when you hit the power button on your device, It will go into a sleep mode instead of being turned off your device or put your device into hibernation. It works just like your phone and other tablets, your Surface will remain connected to the WiFi to receive emails and notifications.

You can save more battery by turning the WiFi off while your device in sleep mode. To do so:

- Go to Settings > System > Power & sleep
- Under the Network connection section, change the value to "Always".

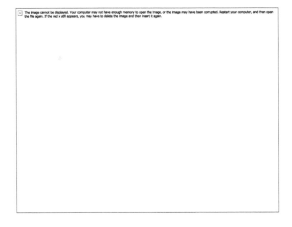

5. Reducing display brightness

Display brightness can use more power than other parts of your computer. For Surface, Microsoft has recommended 25% of brightness for getting longer battery life. You might also need to turn off screen brightness auto adjustment to make sure that the brightness you set is good enough for watching.

To turn off automatic brightness adjustment:

- Go to Settings > System > Display
- Turn off the "Change brightness automatically when lighting changes" option.

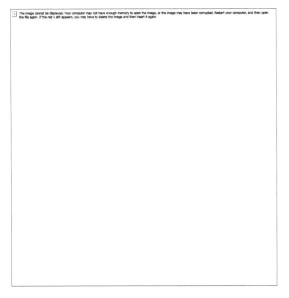

6. Disable startup programs

You can benefit from a faster boot time, reduce your system loads, and save more power juices by disabling unimportant startup programs. To disable startup programs:

- Go to Task Manager

- Click on Start-up.

- Select all programs that you want to disable and click on Disable button.

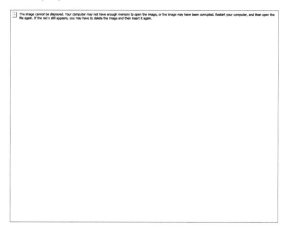

7. Surf with Microsoft Edge

Microsoft Edge is an optimized Web Browser for Windows 10 and also Microsoft Surface. According to a discussion on Reddit, while you viewing videos on the youtube, Microsoft Edge using H.264 codec which allows Intel Skylake processor to natively decode with much less CPU power consumption.

Similarly, for Netflix streaming test that Microsoft conducted on identical Microsoft Surface Books, Microsoft Edge is the best battery efficiency.

Google Chrome Tweaks

However, if you are using Google Chrome you can disable Flash Player plugin and install H264IFY to solve this problem. To disable the flash player plugin:

- Go to Chrome address bar
- Type: "chrome://plugins"
- And click on Disable under the Adobe Flash Player section

- To install h264ify extension, you can go to this URL: https://chrome.google.com/webstore/detail/h264ify/aleakchihdccplidncghkekgioiakgal

8. Turn on Battery Saver

Battery Saver is a new feature in Windows 10, by turning on the Battery Saver option, you can extend your battery life by limiting background system activity and push notifications. You can find the apps that run in the background even you don't use them by going to Settings > System > Battery Saver > Battery use > Change background app settings.

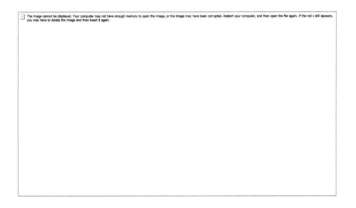

When you turn on Battery Saver option, all those apps will not run in the background. To turn on Battery Saver, you can click on Battery icon on the taskbar and click on Battery saver to turn on.

Note - while your Surface is charging, this option will be disabled.

On Surface PC with Power Slider enabled, you just move the slider all the way to the left to activate the battery saver.

9 Turn off Bluetooth radio

Bluetooth on Surface Pro 4 and Surface Book is a key feature when you are using Surface Pen for OneNote activation, Screenshot, and Cortana activation. However, if you think you don't need these features, you can turn Bluetooth radio off by:

- Go to Settings > Devices > Bluetooth
- And switch off the Bluetooth option

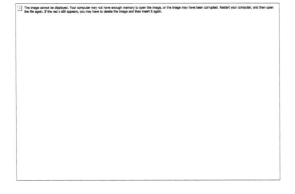

How to charge Surface Pro 7 via USB-C?

It's really simple to charge your Surface Pro 7 via USB-C. Just like the Surface Connect connector, the USB-C connector itself is reversible, so you don't have to worry about the wrong side plug-in. Anyway, there are 2 ways to charge your Surface over USB-C depending on the available charger port:

- USB-A to USB-C: You can charge your Surface Pro 7 with any standard USB charger or portable power bank with a good charging rate (at least 5V/1.5A) by connecting them with the USB-A to USB-C cable.

- USB-C to USB-C: If you have a USB-C PD charger, which is highly recommended, and they are using USB-C port, then you can charge your Surface Pro 7 by connecting them with the USB-C to USB-C cable.

How to Configure Surface Pro UEFI/BIOS Settings

You might already know that since the first generation of Microsoft Surface Pro (2013) and Surface 3, Microsoft has implemented a new firmware called Unified Extensible Firmware Interface (UEFI) on those devices. As this new firmware interface allows your Surface boot faster and providing better security improvements.

Starting with Surface Pro 4, Microsoft has created their own Surface UEFI for using with newer devices. This new Surface UEFI is currently used on newer devices including Surface Book and Surface Studio.

In this section, you will find out how to get to the Surface Pro UEFI settings. You will also see about how to configure the UEFI settings to improve the device security, check your device information and more.

1 How to access Surface Pro UEFI settings?

You can enter Surface Pro UEFI setup screen only while your device is starting up. Here is how you do that:

- Shut down your Surface.

- Press and hold the Volume Up button on your Surface, then press and release the Power button.

- When you see the Surface logo screen appear, release the Volume Up button. The Surface UEFI screen will appear in a few seconds.

How to Enter Surface Pro UEFI/BIOS Settings

After you have made any changes to the UEFI settings, you can restart your Surface by:

- In Surface UEFI menu, choose Exit, and click on Restart Now

How to easily disable adaptive contrast on Surface Pro 7 and Surface Laptop 3

What is *adaptive contrast?*

Adaptive contrast is quite different than auto-brightness (or adaptive brightness), found under Settings > System > Display, and which ramps up and down the display backlight on ambient lighting conditions.

Adaptive contrast differs because it adjusts *based on the current images on your display* rather than the ambient light in your room. It's like "edge-lit local dimming of specific zones" due to what is on the screen. This is also different than High Dynamic Range (HDR), which is much more sophisticated and precise with more color depth.

The feature is standard on modern TVs and high-end gaming monitors, but it can also be a source of frustration. The effect is most noticeable at night when you tend to have a lower display brightness because you are in a dark room.

To simulate the effect, go into a dark room and open Microsoft Word (or anything with a white background) then switch to an app that is all black like Settings (if dark mode is enabled). You should see the screen slowly and smoothly dim and shift in contrast.

Unfortunately, while you can easily disable adaptive brightness under Settings > System > Display > "Change brightness automatically when lighting changes," there is no easy way to disable adaptive contrast. Also, many users conflate the two, but disabling auto- brightness won't solve this behavior if it bothers you.

How to disable adaptive contrast with

Intel's Store app

Intel's Graphics Command Center is a Universal Windows Platform (UWP) app that was released in spring 2019. It is like Intel's Graphic Control Panel but is newer, easier to find, and easier to manage.

1. Go to the **System** tab.
2. Go to the **Power** sub-tab.
3. Turn **Display Power Savings** off.

Likewise, the Intel Graphics Command Center has many options to help tune your display to your liking. You can adjust contrast, sharpness, colors, battery savings, and more. There is no real risk as you can always "revert to default" if your display looks worse, or battery life decreases.

How to Check Your Surface Pro Device Information via UEFI settings?

The first displayed page when you enter UEFI settings is PC information page. On the page, you can find out more information about your device identities such as Model, System UUID (Universally Unique Identifier), Serial Number, and Asset Tag. Moreover, it also displays all important system other components version that you might need for troubleshooting.

How to Configure Device Boot Order on the new Surface Pro

To change the alternate system boot order on your Surface Pro:

- Enter Surface UEFI settings as the instructions above.

- In Surface UEFI menu, go to Boot Configuration page as below: Surface Pro UEFI > Boot Configuration

On the "Configure boot device order" page, you can:

- Rearrange boot order by drag and drop any boot option available in the list.

- Enable or disable any boot option by using the checkbox

- Remove available boot option permanently by using the trash button.

Note if you accidentally delete Windows Boot Manager from your Master Boot Record, simply restart your Surface and Windows Boot Manager will reinstall automatically.

How to Manage Device Components on Surface Pro

Surface Pro allows you to disable some of your surface device components and features to meet your specific security requirements. You can enable or disable those components by:

- Access Surface UEFI settings as the instructions above.

- In Surface UEFI menu, go to Devices and you will see the following options: Surface Pro UEFI > Devices

- In my Surface Pro with System UEFI version 231.1662.769, you can choose to enable or disable the following device's components or ports:

Docking USB Port

Front Camera

Rear Camera

IR Camera

On-board Audio

SDcard

Wi-Fi & Bluetooth

Bluetooth

Type Cover port

How to change your Surface Pro Date and Time via Surface UEFI?

The new Surface UEFI now allows you to set your Surface Pro's date and time right on UEFI settings page. To check or set date and time for your Surface Pro:

- Enter Surface UEFI settings as the instructions above.

- In Surface UEFI menu, go to Date and Time page as below:Surface Pro (2017) UEFI >Date and Time

- To set a new date and time, select the edit box and type your new date and time.

- Press Enter to apply changes.

How to Protect UEFI settings with a password on Surface Pro

You can prevent others from changing your UEFI settings by setting an Administrator Password in UEFI settings. To do that:

- Enter Surface UEFI settings as the instructions above.

- Go to Security section as below: Surface Pro UEFI > Security

- To set UEFI password, click on Add or Change button and you will see the following requirements: Surface Pro UEFI > Add Password

- You will need to enter a password in the box with your keyboard or the on-screen keyboard with following criteria:

Minimum Length: 6 characters

Maximum Length: 128 characters

- May contain a combination of letters, numbers, and special characters.

- In case that you have already set the password before and you want to remove it, simply leave the password box as blank.

Note If you enter the administrator password incorrectly three times, you'll be locked out of the UEFI. Restart your Surface to enter the password again.

Important If you set a password for the UEFI, record it in a safe place. If you forget the password, you won't be able to access the UEFI settings. You can only reset the administrator password from within the UEFI.

Customizing Windows 10

A few customization tweaks can help to make the experience more personal and improve productivity, and in this guide, we show you the way to change the appearance of Windows 10.

Windows 10 ships with a wide range of options to customize the look and feel, with custom lock and desktop backgrounds, color accents, and a variety of settings to tweak the interface, allowing anyone to personalize the experience.

In this Windows 10 guide, we walk you through the steps everyone should know to customize the appearance and make the experience a little more personal.

How to change the desktop background

Perhaps one of the simplest ways to add some personality to your device is to change the desktop background with a custom image or collection of images.

To change your desktop background use these steps:
- Open Settings.
- Click on Personalization.
- Click on Background.

- Using the "Background" drop-down menu, select the Picture option.

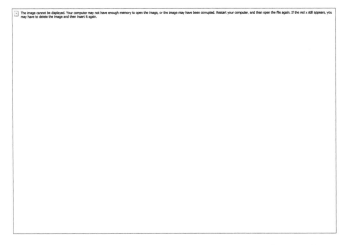

- Click the Browse button to select the image you want to use.
- Using the "Choose a fit" drop-down menu, select the option that best suits the image, including fill, stretch, center, span, etc.

Quick Tip: If you're using a multi-monitor setup, you can use these steps to set a different background for each display.

Setting up a desktop slideshow

If you want to showcase a collection of pictures on the desktop, do the following:

- Open Settings.
- Click on Personalization.
- Click on Background.
- Using the "Background" drop-down menu, select the Slideshow option.

- Click the Browse button to select the folder with the images.
- Use the "Change picture every" drop-down menu to select how often the image will rotate.
- If the order of the images is not important, turn on the Shuffle toggle switch.

- Using the "Choose a fit" drop-down menu, select the option that best suits the images, including fill, stretch, center, span, etc.

How to change the color accent

Windows 10 also lets you change the color accent that appears throughout the experience, including Start, taskbar, Action Center, title bars, and linkable text in apps and Settings.

To change the current color, do the following:
- Open Settings.
- Click on Personalization.
- Click on Colors.
- Select the color accent you want to use through the experience.

Quick Tip: If you want Windows 10 to decide the appropriate color accent, check the Automatically pick an accent color from my background option under "Choose your color."

If the color you want isn't listed, you can click the Custom color button to create a custom color using the palette, or you can click the More button to enter the RGB or HSV code.

Once you found the one you want, simply click the Done button to apply the changes.

Controlling transparency effects

Some elements of Windows 10, such as Start, taskbar, Action Center, and apps include transparency effects with blur and noise textures part of the Microsoft Fluent Design System, and using the Colors page, you can enable or disable these effects using these steps:

- Open Settings.
- Click on Personalization.
- Click on Colors.

- Under "More options," turn on or off the Transparency effects toggle switch.

Adding colors to Windows 10 elements

Windows 10 by default uses a color dark for Start, taskbar, and Action Center, and a light color for title bars. If you want to add a little more personality, it's possible to show the color accent in these elements using these steps:

- Open Settings.
- Click on Personalization.
- Click on Colors.
- Under "More options," check the Start, taskbar, and action center option to show colors in those elements.

- Check the Title bars option to show the color accent in title bars of apps and File Explorer.

Choosing a color mode

Windows 10 includes two personalization modes. The light mode is the default mode and works well during daytime, and then there's the dark mode that uses a dark color scheme in backgrounds and another part of the OS and supported apps, and it's an option more suited for a low-light environment.

You can switch between the light and dark mode using these steps:
- Open Settings.
- Click on Personalization.
- Click on Colors.

- Under "More options," select the Light (default) or Dark using the "Choose your default app mode" option.

If you want to go a step further, you can use our guide to configure your computer to switch between the dark and light mode automatically.

How to customize the Lock screen

Windows 10 also allows you to customize the Lock screen, the screen you slide up every time you turn on your device to get into the sign-in screen.

The options available include the ability to set a custom image, collection of pictures, Windows Spotlight, and settings to control apps notifications.

Lock screen uses "Windows spotlight" as the default option to show a new background every time you turn on your computer, and while this option pulls stunning images from Bing, it's also possible to set any image you want.

To personalize the Lock screen using a custom image, do the following:

- Open Settings.
- Click on Personalization.
- Click on Lock screen.
- Use the "Background" drop-down menu, and select the Picture option.

- Click the Browse button to locate the picture you want to use.

Setting up a Lock screen slideshow

To show a collection of images on the Lock screen, do the following:

- Open Settings.
- Click on Personalization.
- Click on Lock screen.
- Use the "Background" drop-down menu, and select the Slideshow option.
- Click the Add a folder button to locate the folder with the images you want to see.

Additionally, you can click the Advanced slideshow settings link to control other options.

For example, you can include the Camera Roll folders on your device and OneDrive. Choose to use only pictures that are best suited to fit the screen. Allow your computer to show the Lock screen instead of turning off the screen after a certain time of inactivity. And there is a drop-down menu to specify the duration of the slideshow.

On either option you choose, it's also a good idea to turn off the Get fun facts, tips, and more from

Windows and Cortana on your lock screen toggle switch to avoid the so-called "Windows 10 ads" in the lock screen.

Quick Tip: The behavior of Windows 10 is to show the same background on the Lock screen as well as in the Sign-in screen. If you want to see a solid color background in the Sign-in screen make sure to turn off the Show lock screen background picture on the sign-in screen toggle switch listed at the bottom of the page.

Controlling Lock screen app notifications

Some apps can show details and status (such as upcoming calendar events and the number of unseen emails) on the Lock screen. To add or remove the apps that can appear in the experience, do the following:

- Open Settings.
- Click on Personalization.
- Click on Lock screen.

Only one app can show detailed status, which by default is set to the Calendar app. If you want to select another app, click the app button, under Choose an app to show detailed status, to see the available Microsoft Store apps you can pick, or select None to disable the feature.

Using the Choose an app to show quick status option, it's possible to configure up to six apps to includes status on the Lock screen. Usually, you'll see the Mail, Calendar, and Skype apps, but you can always remove, change, or add more apps to the list clicking the app or "+" button.

How to apply a theme

Although Windows 10 includes many ways to personalize your experience, the quickest way to change the look and feel is to use a theme.

A theme is just a package that can contain one or more background images, color accent, and sounds, and they're quickly acquirable from the Microsoft Store.

To get and apply a new theme on Windows 10, do the following:

- Open Settings.
- Click on Personalization.
- Click on Themes.
- Click the Get more themes in the Store link.

- In the Microsoft Store, pick the theme you want, and click the Get button.

- Click the Launch button to go back to the Themes settings.
- Click the newly added theme to apply it.

You can check our guide detailing everything you need to know to manage themes.

How to customize the Start menu

The Start menu is an essential feature of Windows 10, as it's the experience where you can find your apps, settings, and files.

There are a number of ways to customize the Start menu, some of the options can be customized from the menu itself, and additional options can be managed through the Settings app.

Changing basic Start menu settings

You can customize almost everything you see on the menu with the options available through the Start page in the Settings app using these steps:

- Open Settings.
- Click on Personalization.
- Click on Start.

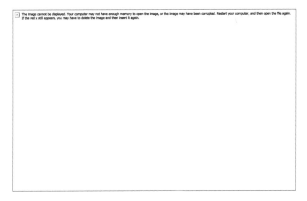

In the Start page, you'll find a number of options you can customize, including:

- Show more tiles on Start — Allows you to add a fourth column of tiles to fit up to 8 (small) tiles in a single row.

- Start menu 3 columns (left), Start menu 4 columns (right)

- Show app list in Start menu — Disabling this option will remove all apps list with only access to your pinned Live Tiles. You can still access your apps clicking the All apps button on the top-left, or typing a search as you open the menu.

- Start menu with all apps list (left), Start menu without all apps list (right)
- Show recently added apps — If you're not interested in seeing the Recently added list, you can turn off this option to remove it.
- Show most used apps — The Start menu lists your more frequently used apps, but you can disable this option if you only want to see all the apps.

- Occasionally show suggestions in Start — When enabled, the Start menu will show recommendations of Microsoft Store, which many consider as ads. You can use this toggle switch to prevent seeing suggestions.

- Start menu with lists (left), Start menu without lists (right)
- Use full screen — enables a Windows 8.1 Start screen-like experience stretching the menu across the desktop letting to see more pinned tiles without having to scroll.

To customize the left rail button, you can click the Choose which folders appear on Start link at the bottom of the page, and then simply turn on or off the toggle switch for the buttons you want to see on the menu.

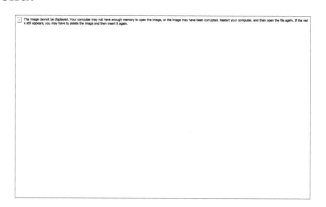

Customizing Live Tiles

Alongside the customization options available through the Settings app, you can also personalize the experience from the menu itself.

Resizing Start

You can resize the menu vertically and horizontally by stretching the edges outwards using the mouse.

Working with tiles, folders, and groups

The Start menu also offers the ability to drag tiles, groups of tiles, and folders anywhere in the menu.

In order to better organize your tiles, you can create a group by dragging tiles into an empty space. You can even click the header of the group to change the name to anything that makes more sense for that group — and yes, emojis are supported.

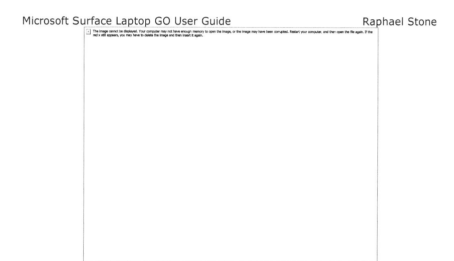

Folders is another way to group tiles inside of tile to optimize the space in the Start menu. You can create new "folders" by dragging and dropping a tile on top of another tile. Then dropping more items into the folder will add them to the group.

Live Tiles and folders support many sizes, which you can change right-clicking a tile, selecting Resize, and choosing from one of the available sizes, including Small, Medium, Wide, or Large.

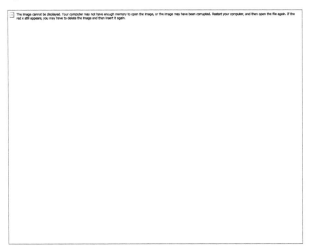

If the live updates isn't a feature you like, right-clicking the tile, and selecting More, you'll find the option to turn off live updates. Also, depending on the app, you will see additional options, such as options to pin or unpin the taskbar, run it with administrator privileges, and more.

A Windows 7 Start menu look

In the case that you prefer a more classic look, you can always remove all the tiles to end up only with the all apps list view, which is a menu very similar to the one found in Windows 7. However, you'll need to right-click each tile and select the Unpin from Start option, as Windows 10 doesn't offer a setting to hide the Live Tile section.

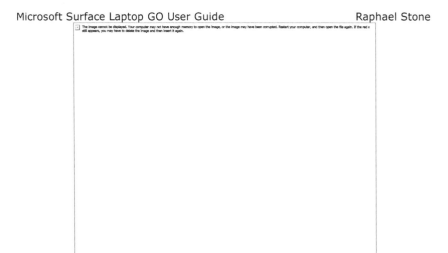

How to customize the taskbar

The taskbar is perhaps one of the features we use the most on Windows 10, and similar to the Start menu, you can customize it in a number of ways using the Settings app and with options available in the taskbar itself.

Changing basic taskbar settings

If you want to customize the taskbar experience, do the following:
- Open Settings.
- Click on Personalization.
- Click on Taskbar.

In this page, it's possible to change many basic options, including:

- Lock the taskbar — If enabled, you can't move or resize the taskbar.
- Automatically hide the taskbar in desktop mode — If enabled, the bar will stay hidden, unless you're actively interacting with it in normal mode.
- Automatically hide the taskbar in tablet mode — If enabled, the bar will stay hidden, unless you're actively interacting with it in tablet mode.

- Use small taskbar buttons — Allows you to use smaller buttons to reduce the footprint of the taskbar.

- Show badges on taskbar buttons — App buttons in the taskbar can show status notifications, and this option lets you disable or enable the feature.

Although you can change the location of the taskbar by just dragging it around with the mouse, this page also includes a drop-down menu to relocate the bar anywhere you like.

In order to customize your experience even further, the taskbar also lets you combine buttons in three different ways, including always combine and hide their labels (default), show labels and combine buttons only when the taskbar is full, and never combine and show buttons labels.

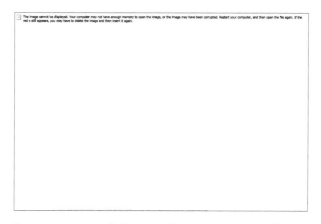

If you have a multi-monitor setup, the Taskbar settings page also includes additional options, such as the ability to show taskbar on all displays, choose where apps button appear, and an option to combine buttons on other taskbars.

Customizing the notification area

In the bottom-right corner of the taskbar, you'll find the notification area, which can quickly get clutter with system and apps icons. However, you can customize the experience to show only the icons you need using these steps:

- Open Settings.
- Click on Personalization.
- Click on Taskbar.
- Under "Notification area," click the Select which icons appear on the taskbar link.

- Turn on the toggle switch for each icon you want to appear in the bottom-right corner of the screen.

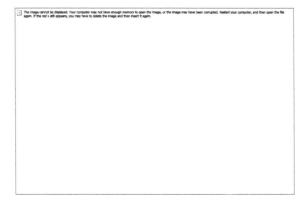

- Under "Notification area," click the Turn system icons on or off link.

- Turn on the toggle switch for each system icons (such as Clock, Volume, and Network) that will appear in the bottom-right corner of the screen.

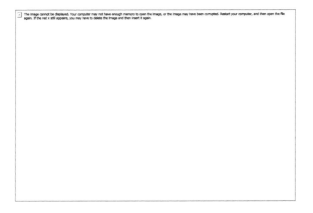

Disabling My People

My People is a new experience that makes it easier to connect with people you know, but if it's a feature you don't use, you can quickly disable it using these steps:

- Open Settings.
- Click on Personalization.
- Click on Taskbar.
- Under "People," turn off the Show contacts on the taskbar toggle switch.

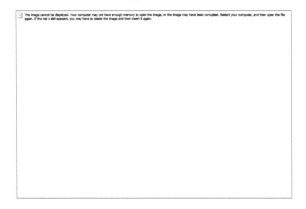

Optimizing the taskbar space

Alongside the customization options available through the Settings app, you can change a few other options from the taskbar itself.

For example, if you don't actively use the Cortana search box, you can remove it or show only a button to access the experience to get more space to pin additional apps.

To remove the search box, you can right-click the taskbar, select Cortana, and click the Hidden option, or you can also select the Show Cortana icon option.

Using the same taskbar context menu, you can remove the Task View, People, and other buttons which could just be wasting valuable space in the bar.

You can also check this guide for more details on how to fully optimize the space on the taskbar.

Wrapping things up

Although the default options should be adequate for most users, Windows 10 provides a slew of customization settings to change the look and feel that helps to make the experience more personal without having to resource to third-party tools or hacks.

This guide is focused on changing the personalization options that most people will use, but it's worth noting that there are many other ways and features you can customize on Windows 10.

Microsoft Edge Web Browser

Let's face it, Internet Explorer has always been the butt of jokes when surfing the web. It's slow, clunky and full of security holes and has since the beginning.

While Microsoft has invested over the last few years in IE to make it better, it just seemed they couldn't get away from the stigma associated with their flagship browser. That's where Microsoft Edge comes in.

Edge is Microsoft's new flagship browser. Let's take a look at how to get started with Edge, what you can do with it and why you should give it a shot.

What You Need to Know About Edge

It should come as no surprise that Edge comes as the default browser in Windows 10. In fact, regardless of what browser was default before you upgrade, you'll find that it's automatically switched to Edge in Windows 10. You can easily switch it back with our guide here.

Edge originally went by the codename Project Spartan before the Windows 10 release. Edge is leaps and bounds above Internet Explorer in just about every way and on a clean install in Windows 10 can even outperform Chrome and Firefox out of the box.

It's still missing some key features, like add-on support which Microsoft claims is "coming soon." (sometime during the 1st half of 2016). There's still render issues with certain websites and flash support, but more and more websites are getting used to coding to include Edge, too.

Getting Started with Edge

You'll find the Edge icon in the Start Menu after installing or upgrading to Windows 10. Simply click on it to get started.

When you open Edge for the first time, you'll be greeted by and introduction to Microsoft's new browser. From there, you'll notice Edge takes on the appearance of a Windows 10 universal app with clean lines, colors and a Start Screen-esque layout. It takes some time to get used to but if you used Windows 8 and 8.1, it'll be a quick adaptation.

If you're logged into a Microsoft Account, you'll notice you're automatically logged into it in Edge, too.

In the upper right-hand corner, you'll find access to settings, Cortana note taking, sharing, along with bookmarks and favorites. These are in the toolbar and easy to access, making Edge more intuitive to work with than IE ever was.

By clicking on the "Settings" icon, you'll have access to even more in Edge, including InPrivate browsing, a holdout from IE which works just the same for users looking to go undercover on the web.

You'll be able to pin websites to the Start Menu from here, along with accessing search, print and developer tools. You can also open IE directly from Edge, which allows you to open the same page you've navigated to in Microsoft's old browser.

You can also Send feedback form the Edge settings menu, something I recommend you take advantage of whenever you have issues or want to see features added to Edge.

Now, click on "Settings" from the settings menu.

Edge has simplified settings for the browser, making it easier to customize and change key ways the browser works. We recommend taking a walk-through the settings, tweaking what you want and getting to know Edge as a browser in Windows 10.

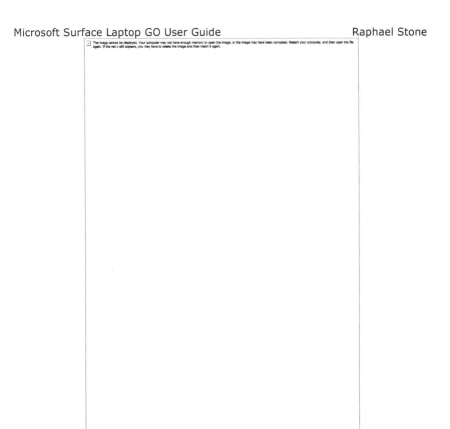

For now, Edge only works in Windows 10. There's no telling whether Microsoft will make it available for other versions of Windows in the future.

IE, for the time being, will still be included, updated and part of the Windows OS.

Turning Off Flash in Edge

Flash has become a growing concern among web users over the last few years due to security flaws and just the overall outdated system of using flash online.

Here's the steps you need to take to turn off Flash in Edge.

- Open "Settings" in Edge.

- Scroll to the bottom and click on "View advanced settings."

- Click the slider to turn off Flash under "Use Adobe Flash Player."

- Restart the browser and Flash will be disabled until you turn it back on yourself.

Conclusion

There's still room for improvement in Edge but it runs better and smoother than IE ever did. If you're looking to give Edge a chance, do so and keep an open mind. It took Microsoft a lot to give up the "Internet Explorer" name in Windows 10.

It's clear Microsoft gets they can't keep letting consumers utilize a browser that's stuck in the 1990s. Edge is a leap forward, and while there's room for more key changes, it looks like Microsoft is taking a step in the right direction. Give Edge a try, you might be surprised by the results.

Thank you for purchasing our book!

Printed in the USA
CPSIA information can be obtained
at www.ICGtesting.com
LVHW070725091223
766096LV00012B/681